MACHINE LEARNING

Master Machine Learning for Aspiring Data Scientists

MG Martin

TABLE OF CONTENTS

Introduction

Many people consider machine learning to be the road to riches, the road that leads to artificial intelligence. And it may well be, but for data scientists, for businessmen, and for statisticians, it the most powerful tool at their disposal, a tool that allows them to achieve predictive results of an unprecedented level.

Before we dive into the whys and wherefores of machine learning for data science, it is worth spending a bit of time talking about why it is so important. Most people already know something about artificial intelligence and normally when we hear about it, we think of robots doing the same things that humans do. It is important to understand that, while there are easy tasks, there are also difficult ones and a time when robots take over most human tasks is a long way off.

However, machine learning is here, and it is here to stay. Artificial intelligence is a branch of machine learning and just about every AI task is based on machine learning. Not so long ago, there was a common belief that robots would need to learn everything they know from humans. The human brain is a highly sophisticated organ and it isn't easy to describe every action it co-ordinates. In 1959 Arthur Samuel came up with the idea that, rather than teaching computers, we could make them learn instead. He was also responsible for the term 'machine learning' and now, whenever we talk of machine learning, we are referring to computers learning tasks autonomously.

Some examples of machine learning that some people may not realize are machine learning include:

1. **Natural Language Processing** – otherwise called NLP. A good example of this is translation apps, such as Google

Translate. This isn't backed by a standard dictionary, it is a set of algorithms that updates itself based on the way different words are used.

2. **Voice Assistants** – such as Alexa, Siri, Google Assistant, and Cortana. These are all examples of technologies based on speech recognition and all of them are built on machine learning algorithms.

3. **Spam Filters** – every email provider has a spam filter, keeping unwanted email out of your inbox. Machine learning algorithms are used to learn what is and isn't spam, learning better as they filter more emails.

4. **Recommendation Systems** – you see it on Amazon, Netflix, YouTube, even Facebook. All recommendations are made based on your search activity, behavior, likes, follows, and more. No human could ever produce recommendations as well-suited and, while there are those who believe it to be intrusive, this is the type of data that is far too complex for humans to process. Machines match sellers and buyers, books with readers, movies with viewers and more. And Amazon has taken things even further. The algorithms they use are so good, they can pretty much predict what you will buy and when and they are so confident of that, they will send the product to the warehouse nearest you, allowing you to get it same or next day as you order it.

Some machine learning instances that are already here revolve around the financial sector. Machine learning algorithms can do what humans can't – they can respond to changes in the market quicker than you can even think about it.

You can predict whether an employee is likely to leave for another job, whether a customer will buy or go to a competitor, or just not make any purchase at all. Sales can be predicted, hidden opportunities uncovered, and so much more. Machine learning opens the door to a multitude of opportunities and there is no end in sight to what it can do.

And then we have the self-drive cars, something that we only saw in films until just recently. Now, millions of miles have been covered by these cars and it was all done using algorithms that allow the car to learn how to drive efficiently and safely.

I could go on and on but I won't. I'm sure you can see why machine learning is so important so, what I am going to discuss here is the process behind it. There will be a few code examples but not many – this is mostly theory but I have tried to keep it light-hearted. I covered much of the practical side in my other books so, for this book, you should have a good idea as to what to expect. If you read those guides, you will have the experience necessary to start this one so I suggest that you work through this guide using your own data.

Data Science is a tough field to get into and mastering machine learning is a vital part of that field.

Chapter 1

A Look at Machine Learning Algorithms

Before we can really get started on our journey, we need to clear up a huge misconception that surrounds machine learning – it is NOT about algorithms.

Open any syllabus or university textbook and you will be confronted with a long list of algorithms and that is one of the fuels igniting the misconception. Yes, you do need to learn lots of different algorithms but machine learning is about so much more.

It is one of the most comprehensive approaches to problem-solving and each algorithm is just one tiny part of that puzzle. For the most part, the puzzle is all about applying those algorithms in the right way to get the right result.

Why is Machine Learning So Special?

Break it down and machine learning is about nothing more than teaching a computer to identify and learn patterns from the data you give it. Often, that is for the purpose of making predictions or decisions. And for real machine learning, the computer has got to be able to learn patterns it hasn't been programmed explicitly to identify.

Let's take a famous example, a curious child.

A young boy is playing in his home; there is a candle burning in the table so he goes towards it.

1. He is curious, so he puts his hand over the flame

2. He yells in pain, pulling his hand back

3. He identifies that the bright red thing hurt him

A couple of days later, he is playing in the kitchen. The stovetop is on so he goes toward it again.

- Curious once more, he thinks about putting his hand over it again

- Then he notices that it is bright red

- He hesitates and pulls back, remembering that bright red means pain and he doesn't put his hand over it.

This is a basic form of machine learning – the young boy learned patterns from the candle and his own actions. Because he remembered that the bright red candle flame hurt him, he avoided putting his hand over the stovetop, which was also glowing bright red. However, had he avoided the stovetop because he was told to by his parents, that would be classed as explicit programming and not machine learning.

Key Terminology

What I want to focus on for now is a practical achievement, rather than getting bogged down in technicalities. There is plenty of time for that later. As such, it is important that you understand the terminology. These are the terms you need to be aware of:

- **Model** – a pattern set learned from specific data

- **Algorithm** – a machine learning process used for training the model

- **Training Data** – the dataset the algorithm learns from

- **Test Data** – a subset of the dataset set aside to evaluate the performance of the model

- **Features** – columns, or variables, within the dataset; these are used for training the model

- **Target Variable** – a variable that you are attempting to predict

- **Observations** – the data points, or rows, in the dataset

Let's take an example of a dataset containing information about 150 primary school students. You want to make predictions on their Height, based on Gender, Age, and Weight:

A) There are 150 observations in the dataset

B) There is one target variable, which is Height

C) There are three features, which are Age, Gender, Weight

Your dataset will be split into two subsets:

A) 120 observations used for training models on – this is known as the training set

B) 30 observations used for evaluating and choosing the best model – this is known as the test set.

We'll go into this in more detail in a later chapter.

Machine Learning Tasks

Academic machine learning begins with algorithms and it focuses on them. With applied machine learning, the important thing is choosing the right algorithm for the task at hand.

A) A task is a specified objective for the algorithm

B) You can swap algorithms in and out, so long as you have the right task

C) Always try several algorithms because, to start with, you will not know which is the right one for the task

Machine learning tasks are separated into a number of categories, with the two most common ones being supervised learning and unsupervised learning.

Supervised Learning

This includes tasks for what is known as labeled data. That means we have a target variable.

A) In practice, supervised learning is generally used as a more advanced method of predictive modeling.

B) Every observation has to be labeled with an answer that is 'correct'

C) Then, and only then, can you build your predictive model. The algorithm must be told what is right while it is being trained, hence the term, 'supervised'.

D) We use regression to model continuous target variables

E) We use classification to model categorical or class target variables

Unsupervised Learning

Unsupervised learning revolves around tasks that have unlabeled data, which means there is no target variable.

A) In practice, unsupervised learning is generally used as a kind of automated signal extraction or automated data analysis.

B) There is no predetermined 'correct' order

C) The algorithm learns patterns from the data directly, with no supervision

D) The most common of the unsupervised learning tasks is clustering, used for identifying groups in data.

The Three Main Elements of Really Good Machine Learning

To build effective machine learning models, and build them consistently, to give you good results, there are three main elements:

A) **A top-class chef – human guidance**

Although the idea is to teach a computer to learn by itself, human guidance is still a very big factor and, as you will come to see, humans are required to make many decisions, the first one is to decide how your project should be road mapped to guarantee success.

B) **Fresh ingredients – relevant and clean data**

This is all about the quality of data – regardless of which algorithm you use, always stick with the principle of Garbage In = Garbage Out. Most data scientists will spend more time cleaning their data, understanding it and engineering features than they do on the actual models.

C) Don't overcook things – don't over fit your data

Over fitting is an incredibly dangerous machine learning pitfall because models that are over fitted have memorized noise in your training set rather than learning what the underlying patterns are. For example, if a hedge fund has an over fit model it could cause losses totaling millions of dollars; for a hospital, it could cost many lives. Of course, most applications won't have such high stakes but it still remains that over fitting is a huge mistake.

We will go over all of this in the course of this book and, by the end, you will understand everything.

The Machine Learning Blueprint

All machine learning journeys follow are based on those three elements and they all follow five fundamental steps:

A) **Exploratory Analysis** - getting to know the data – this should be a quick step, very efficient

B) **Data Cleaning** – your data must then be cleaned – keep in mind that better data will always beat fancy algorithms

C) **Feature Engineering** – next, you need to give your data helping hand in focusing on the important stuff and you do this by creating some new features

D) **Algorithm Selection** – find and select the best algorithms for the task

E) **Model Training** – lastly, you can train the model.

There are a few other steps that you might need to do as well:

A) **Project Scoping** - you may need to roadmap your project and anticipate your data requirements

B) **Data Wrangling** – your dataset might need to be restructured into a format that can be handled by the algorithms

C) **Preprocessing** – sometimes, you can make your model perform much better if you transform the features first

D) **Ensembling** – and if you combine several models together, you can enhance performance even more.

We'll be focusing on the five main steps – these ones will slot in quite nicely when you understand the workflow.

Chapter 2

Exploratory Analysis

In the first chapter, we took a brief look at machine learning and the path, as a data scientist, you will take. As you saw, most data science revolves around five main steps and this is where we start looking at those steps.

The first is exploratory analysis and you should NOT get this mixed up with summary statistics or data visualization. Those two are nothing more than tools, a means to an end.

Exploratory analysis is all about getting the answers to questions. It is all about extracting sufficient insights out of the data to make sure you are on the correct path and in this chapter we are going to look at which insights you should be looking for.

Why You Need to Explore Your Dataset First

Explanatory analysis has one fundamental purpose – to get to know your data. Making it the first job you do will make the rest of your project run much smoother in these three ways:

- You get some valuable tips for cleaning your data and these can either make your model or break it.

- You get some ideas for engineering the features, and these can take your model from being good to being truly great.

- You get a feel for your data and this helps you to communicate the results and deliver a much bigger impact with your model.

The one thing, the most important thing, about exploratory analysis is that it should be fast. It must be efficient and it must be decisive.

Never leave this step out but don't dwell on it for too long either. There are tons of possible charts, plots and tables but you really only need to use a small handful of them to get to know your data sufficiently well.

In this first real lesson, we'll look at the best visualizations for the data.

The Basics Come First

The first thing to do is get the answers to some basic questions regarding your dataset:

A) How many observations are in the dataset?

B) How many features does the dataset have?

C) What data types are the features? Categorical? Numerical?

D) Is there a target variable?

Example Observations

The next thing you will want to do is display some sample observations from your dataset. This gives you a feel for each feature's values and it is a good way of making sure it all makes sense. You are not doing any rigorous analysis here, you are just looking for the answers to questions like these:

A) Do the columns look right? Make sense?

B) What about the values in those columns? Do they make sense?

C) Are the values scaled correctly?

D) Do you think that missing data will cause a problem?

Plotting Numerical Distributions

Next, you should plot the numeric feature distributions and, more often than not, the best way to do that is to use a standard grid of histograms. Some of the things you want to look out for include:

A) Unexpected distributions

B) Potential outliers that make no sense

C) Features that really should be binary

D) Boundaries that make no sense

E) Potential errors in measurements

This is the point where, if you haven't been already, you should be noting down any potential fixes. If something doesn't look right, like a potential outlier in a feature, now is a good time to dig a little bit deeper.

However, we won't be making any fixes until we get to the data cleaning step just so that we can keep everything organized.

Plotting Categorical Distributions

You cannot visualize categorical features via a histogram but you can by using a bar plot. What you want to be looking out for here is any class that might have a sparse class – this is a class that only has a few observations.

As an aside, classes are just unique values for categorical features. As an example, let's say that you had a feature named exterior walls; things like Stucco, Siding, and Brick would all be classes for the feature.

Look on the bar chart for very short bars – these are the sparse classes and they can cause problems when it comes to building the model. In the best-case scenario, they won't have much influence over a model and, in the worst case, they can cause over fitting.

One recommendation I would make is that you consider reassigning or combining some of the classes but we'll leave this until we get to the chapter on feature engineering.

Plotting Segmentations

Segmentation is one of the most powerful ways of exploring the relationship between numeric and categorical features. A box plot lets you do this. For example, working with the real-estate dataset, you could draw several insights, including:

1. Media transaction price

2. Min and max transaction prices

3. Round-number min and max – could indicate truncation

That last point is an important one to remember when you look at generalization later on.

Studying the Correlations

Lastly, you should study the correlations. These allow you to see relationships between the numeric features and the other numeric features. Correlations are representative of the way that features move in unison and are values between -1 and 1. There isn't any need to remember any math for calculating them; you just need to know that:

A) A positive correlation is telling you that two features will increase together. For example, age and height in a child

B) A negative correlation is telling you that, as a feature increases, so another decreases. For example, how many hours are spent studying against how many parties are attended

C) A correlation that is close to -1 or 1 is indicating a stronger relationship

D) A correlation close to 0 is indicating a weaker relationship

E) A correlation at exactly 0 is indicating there is no relationship

You can use visualize this using a correlation heat map and, generally you should be looking for:

A) The features that have a strong correlation to the target variable

B) Whether there are any unexpected or interesting strong correlations between any of the other features.

Once again, your goal is to gain insights, to get a feel for the data and this will assist you as you go through the rest of the machine learning data flow. By the time you have finished doing the exploratory analysis, you will have gained a good idea about your dataset, a few ideas for data cleaning, and maybe some ideas for when it comes to engineering the features.

In the next chapter, I will walk you through data cleaning.

Chapter 3

Data Cleaning

In the last chapter, we cast our eye over some data visualization techniques that help with exploratory analysis and we also looked at what insights you should be keeping your eye out for. Based on what you found using your own data, it's now time to get your data into shape and we do that by doing some data cleaning.

This varies with each different dataset so we can't possibly cover every single thing you may potentially come across. However, you can use this guide as a starting point, a framework that you can use every time. We look at some of the more common steps, like how to handle missing data, how to fix structural errors and how to filer observations.

Let's start cleaning the data.

Better Data Is Worth More than Fancy Algorithms

Data cleaning is one of those jobs that all data scientists do but none of them really talk about it. It isn't the nicest bit of machine learning and there are no hidden secrets or tricks to it. But it is the one step that can either make your project or break it completely and the professionals in the data science community tend to spend rather a long time on it.

Why?

Look at the title of this section – better data is worth more than fancy algorithms. That is one of the simplest machine learning truths and there is no getting away from it.

In simple terms, garbage in will definitely equal garbage out. If you forget everything else you ever learned, do not forget this point.

If your dataset is cleaned properly, even the simplest of algorithms can learn some impressive and useful insights from it. Obviously, the type of cleaning you do will depend on the dataset but you can use the approach in this section as your starting point every time.

Remove any Unwanted Observations

This is the first step in cleaning your data – getting rid of any observations you don't need in your dataset, and that includes those that have been duplicated, triplicated, or more.

Duplicate Observations – these tend to arise the most during the data collection phase usually when you:

- Combine two or more datasets from different places

- Scrape the data

- Get data from other departments or clients

Irrelevant Observations – these do not fit the problem you want to solve:

- If, for example, you wanted a model built around Single-Family homes, you would need observations for Duplexes or Apartments

- This would also be a good time to look back at the charts you produced during exploratory analysis; look for the categorical features and see if any classes stand out as irrelevant

- Doing all this before you get to feature engineering can save time and headaches.

Fixing the Structural Errors

The next step is to fix any structural errors, those that appear when you are transferring data, doing measurements, or any other type of housekeeping that could be considered as poor. For example, check for inconsistency in capitalization, or typographical errors.

This will mostly be an issue for categorical features and looking at your bar plots will give you a good idea of what needs to be done.

After you correct the errors, you will see that the class distribution is significantly cleaner. You should also check that your classes have not been mislabeled too, for example, two or more individual classes that should be the same:

- If, for example, you have Not Applicable and N/A are two classes, combine them into one

- Classes called information technology and IT should also be one class.

Filter the Unwanted Outliers

Outliers can be problematic with certain model types, i.e. regression models don't do as well with outliers as decision tree models do. Generally, if your reasons for removing an outlier are legitimate, the performance of your model will improve.

However you do need to keep in mind that an outlier is quite innocent until you have proven its guilt. Never, ever remove one for stupid reasons, like it's a big number – that number could be providing quite a lot of information to the model.

This really cannot be said enough – outliers should be left where they are unless you have a very good reason for getting rid of them, perhaps suspicious measurements that are most likely not real data.

Handling Missing Data

Missing data is quite tricky, deceptively so, when it comes to applied machine learning. The first thing I need to make clear to you is that, if there are values missing from the dataset, you cannot ignore them. They must be handled for one excellent reason – algorithms will not accept any missing values.

Unfortunately, the two ways that are recommended for missing data are actually not that good. Those methods are:

- Dropping the observations that have got missing values

- Imputing the values using other observations as the basis

The first option, dropping the values, is not good for the model; when you drop an observation, you are losing information. And in fact, it could be quite informative that the data was missing in the first place. Also, in real-world problems, you will most likely be making predictions on data even when there are missing values.

The second option, imputing the values, is also not good for the model because, when you fill in a missing value, you will always lose information, regardless of the sophistication of your imputation method. Again, the fact that there is a missing value is often quite telling and you should always inform the algorithm of missing values. Plus, even if your model is built with imputation in mind, you are not adding new information; all you do is reinforce the patterns that are already there from the other features.

The simple answer is that, because the missing value is information in itself, you should tell the algorithm that it is missing. The question is, how?

- **Missing Categorical Data**

If you have missing data in your categorical features, the easiest way is to give them a label of Missing. What you are doing is putting in a new class for the categorical feature, at the same time as informing the algorithm that there is a missing value and it gets around the issue that algorithms cannot have missing values.

- **Missing Numeric Data**

Where you have numeric data missing, the values should be flagged and filled. The observation should be flagged with a variable indicating that the value is missing and the original value filled with 0; again, this meets the requirements surrounding algorithms and values.

Using this technique allows the algorithm to estimate what the optima missingness constant should be rather than using the mean to fill it.

Once you have completed this step, your dataset will be robust enough that it can skirt around most of the common issues.

In the next chapter, we take a look at feature engineering.

Chapter 4

Feature Engineering

We've looked at reliable ways of cleaning datasets, handling missing data, fixing structural errors and filtering observations. Now we need to take a look at feature engineering, to see how we can give the algorithm some help and bring about improvements to performance. It is worth bearing in mind that this is the step data scientists tend to spend the most amount of time on.

What is Feature Engineering?

Feature engineering is all about taking your existing features and creating new ones from them. The data cleaning process is one of subtracting and then adding new features and it could be one of the most valuable things any data scientist will do to make their model perform better. There are three major reasons for this:

1. Key information can be isolated and highlighted and this can help algorithms to focus on the important stuff.

2. Data scientists can introduce domain expertise

3. Once you grasp the feature engineering 'vocabulary' you can bring in domain expertise from others.

What we will look at in this chapter is some of the heuristics you can use to create new ideas but, before we move on, you should know that this is only a small sample of what you can do – feature engineering is pretty much limitless in nature. However, the more experience you gain, the better you will get at this step.

Infusing Domain Knowledge

Very often, informative features can be engineered by making use of domain expertise, either yours or someone else's. Think of some of the information that you might want isolated – we'll use the real-estate dataset as an example here, using the housing crisis.

Let's say that you have a suspicion that house prices are going to be affected; an indicator variable could be created for any transaction during a set period. These are binary variables and they have one of two values – 0 or 1. They are used to indicate whether observations meet specific conditions and can also be used for isolating some key properties.

Domain expertise is quite broad and is definitely open-ended. At some point you will run out of ideas and that is where these next steps can help, a few very specific heuristics you can use for sparking ideas.

Creating Interaction Features

The first is to see if there are any interaction features that you can create. Interaction features combine two or more features. There are contexts where an interaction term has to be the product from two variables and, in the context we are using they may be sums, products, even differences between features. Generally, it is useful to look at pairs of features and see if you can combine the information in them in a useful way.

Using the real-estate example:

- Let's assume that we have a feature named num_schools – this indicates how many schools are in a 5-mile radius of a property

- We have a feature named median_school – this indicates the median quality score for the schools

- However, we may have suspicions that the most important factor is having many options for school but only good options.

- To capture an interaction like that we would engineer a new feature names school_score = num_schools x median_school.

Combining Sparse Classes

The next heuristic is to group sparse classes together. As far as categorical features go, a sparse class is one that doesn't have many observations and these can cause problems for some machine learning algorithms and lead to over fitting.

Things to remember include:

- There aren't any formal rules on the minimum number of observations per class

- It is dependent on the dataset size and how many other features you have

- A rule of thumb is to combine classes until each has got ~50 observations but this is just a guideline.

Back to our real-estate example.

To start with, similar classes can be grouped. If you download the dataset and look at it you will see that the feature called exterior_walls has a number of similar classes. You could consider grouping classes such as Wood, Wood Shingle and Wood Siding into one class you could label as Wood.

Then you can go through and group together all the other sparse classes into one class named "Other" - you can do this even if you already have a class called "Other." Some of the classes that could go into it at Stucco, Concrete Block, Other, Masonry, Asbestos Shingle, etc.

Once all the sparse classes are combined, you are left with a handful of unique classes, all of which have more observations.

Adding Dummy Variables

There are few algorithms that can handle categorical features directly so you these features need some dummy variables. A dummy variable is a set of binary variables, with 0 or 1 values, each representative of one class from a feature.

You are representing the exact same information but by using a numeric representation, you can pass the algorithm's technical requirements. After we group the sparse classes from the real-estate dataset, we are left with these classes, each translating to a dummy variable:

Original Class	Dummy Variable
Wood	exterior_walls_Wood
Brick	exterior_walls_Brick
Other	exterior_walls_Other

Siding (Alum/Vinyl)	exterior_walls_Siding (Alum/Vinyl)
Missing	exterior_walls_Missing
Metal	exterior_walls_Metal
Brick Veneer	exterior_walls_Brick Veneer
Combination	exterior_walls_Combination

Removing Unused Features

The last step is to get rid of any redundant or unused features. Unused features are the features where it doesn't make any sense to pass them to the algorithm, such as ID columns, some text descriptions or those that aren't there when the prediction is made. The redundant features are those that tend to be replaced by other features added during the engineering phase.

Once the data cleaning and engineering stages are complete, your dataset has been transformed int an ABT – analytical base table – and this is what your model will be built on.

Don't expect all your features to be great; some will make no difference to your model but that doesn't matter – one great predictive feature is worth 10 bad ones any day of the week. The key lies in choosing an algorithm that can choose the best features automatically from multiple options, thus avoiding over fitting.

In the next chapter, we look at selecting algorithms.

Chapter 5

Algorithm Selection

In this section of the guide, we are going to look at selecting the algorithms. Rather than discussing every one of them – there are a lot – we're just going to look at best practices.

There are two very powerful mechanisms in the modern machine learning algorithm – regularization and ensembles – and both fix flaws in older algorithms.

How to Choose an Algorithm

We're going to look at five algorithms, all different, for regression and at their classification counterparts too. Where applied machine learning is concerned, algorithms should be swapped with one another depending on what gives the best performance for the dataset and the problem. The focus here will be on practical benefit and intuition more than theory and math.

Why is Linear Regression Flawed?

Basic linear regression is one of the most common models yet it has some serious flaws. Simple linear regression fits straight lines and, in practice, they don't perform very well at all. In fact, you are best forgetting them for most problems. The biggest advantage is that they are easily understood and interpreted but our goal isn't to produce a research report after studying the data; it is to produce an accurate prediction model. For this, simple linear regression has two big flaws:

1. It is prone to over fitting when there are a lot of input features

2. It doesn't express non-linear relationships very easily

The first flaw is addressed easily.

Machine Learning Regularization

Regularization is considered to be advanced in many ways but it is quite easy to understand. So, the first flaw is the issue of over fitting when there are many features. An example will help us understand why this happens:

- Let's assume that our training dataset has 100 observations

- We also have 100 features

- If a linear regression model is fit with all the features, the training set can be memorized perfectly

- Every coefficient would memorize a single observation and there would be 100% accuracy on training data – it's a different matter for unseen data, though

- The model will not have learned the underlying patterns, learning only the noise from the training data.

Regularization is one of the techniques used to prevent the over fitting and it does this by artificially penalizing all the model coefficients.

- It dampens large coefficients, thus discouraging them

- It sets coefficients to 0, thus removing some features altogether

- The penalty 'strength' is tunable – more on this later.

Regularized Regression Algorithms

There are three types of these:

Lasso Regression

Least Absolute Shrinkage and Selection Operator – Lasso – penalizes the coefficient's absolute size. In practical terms this leads to coefficients with a value of exactly 0. As such, because some features can be removed completely, Lasso offers automatic feature selection. Don't forget that the penalty strength should be tuned and stronger penalties lead to more zero coefficients.

Ridge Regression

Ridge regression will penalize the coefficient's squared size and, in practical terms, this results in smaller coefficients, although they are not forced to 0. In simple terms, ridge regression will offer feature shrinkage. Again, you should tune the penalty strength and stronger penalties will lead to coefficients being pushed nearer to zero.

Elastic-Net

Elastic-net provides a compromise between the Ridge and the Lasso regression. This one will penalize a combination of squared and absolute coefficient sizes and the ratio between the penalty types needs to be tuned, as does the overall strength.

There isn't a best penalty type; it all comes down to the problem and the dataset. You should try out different algorithms using a range of strengths as part of your tuning process – see chapter 6.

Decision Tree Algorithms

So, we looked at three different algorithms, all protecting linear regression from the problem of over fitting but in case you forget, there is a second flaw that affects linear regression – the problem of not being able to express non-linear relationships very easily.

Addressing that requires that we move away from linear regression and that means a new algorithm category.

A decision tree will model the data as a kind of tree containing hierarchical branches. These branches continue to be made until they get to leaves, representing each prediction.

Because a decision has a branching structure they can be used for modeling the non-linear relationships. Staying with the real-estate example:

- Let's say that, as far as Single Family Homes are concerned, the larger the lot, the higher the price

- However, with Apartments, the smaller lots have higher prices

- This is a correlation reversal that linear models struggle to capture unless an interaction term is explicitly added and, for that, you need to anticipate it from the start

- Decision trees can capture the correlation reversal relationship easily.

However, the decision tree is not perfect and has one big flaw too. Allowing the "grow without limits" will result in them memorizing the training data and that, in turn, results in ever more branches.

In short, a decision tree without constraints is also prone to over fitting. So how do we use the flexibility that a decision tree provides without letting them over fit the training data?

Tree Ensembles

An ensemble is a machine learning method that allows predictions to be combined from several models. There are two very common ensembling methods:

- **Bagging** - this tries to reduce the chances of over fitting with complex models. It does this by training more strong learners in parallel with one another. Strong learners are unconstrained models; these are all combined together to smooth the predictions out.

- **Boosting** – this tries to improve the predictive flexibility in the simpler models. It does this by training a sequence of weak learners, which are constrained models (the maximum depth of each tree can be limited). Each of the learners will focus on learning from mistakes made by the one that came before it and boosting will them combine the weak learners to make one strong learner.

Both of these are ensemble methods and both approach the same problem but from opposite directions. Where bagging attempts to smooth the predictions using complex base models, boosting attempts to boost the aggregate complexity of simple base models.

Ensembling is a very general term but when a base model is a decision tree, it is called either a boosted tree or a random forest.

Random Forests

A random forest is when large numbers of decision trees (strong ones) are trained and their predictions combined using bagging. There are also two randomness sources for the random forest:

- Each tree in the forest can choose only from one random feature subset to split on – this leads to feature selection

- Each tree can only be trained on a random observation subset in a process called resampling.

In practical terms, random forests work well out of the box, beating models that can take weeks to develop. They get good results pretty much all of the time and there are few tough parameters for tuning.

Boosted Trees

Opposite to the random forest, the boosted tree trains sequence of weak decision trees, using bosting to combine the predictions.

- Each tree is allowed to go to a maximum depth and this must be tuned

- Each tree will attempt to correct prediction errors from the tree before it.

In practical terms, boosted trees have very high ceilings of performance and, following correct tuning, they tend to beat a lot of other models. They are, however, very complicated to tune, more so than the random forest.

What you should take away from all this is that the best algorithms will offer a mixture of automatic feature selection, regularization, non-linear relationship expression and/or ensembling. Those algorithms include:

- Ridge regression

- Lasso regression

- Elastic-Net

- Random forest

- Boosted tree

Chapter 6

Training the Model

We have reached the final step, training the model. The hardest part is done with the cleaning and the feature engineering so training, or fitting, the model is relatively easy. We're going to discuss some techniques that have become best practice.

How to Train a Machine Learning Model

You might feel as though it took time to get to this stage but a good data scientist will spend most of their time on the every step that leads to this one. What this chapter will cover is setting up the process to ensure maximum performance for your model while preventing over fitting.

Split the Dataset

We'll begin with a very important step that often gets overlooked – spending the data. Your data should be thought of as being a resource in limited supply. Some can be spent on training the model, which means giving it to your algorithm, and some can be spent on evaluating or testing the model. What you can't do is use the same data for the two sets.

If you were to train your model and then use the same data for testing it, your model would most likely be incredibly over fitted and you wouldn't see it. Models have to be judged on their capabilities of predicting new data, unseen data. That means you need to split your dataset into two – a training set and a test set.

The training set is used for fitting and tuning the model whereas the test set is unseen data, new data that your model will be tested on. So, the very first thing you need to do is split the dataset otherwise you will not get very reliable estimates of the way your model performs. Once you have split the dataset, you must not touch the test data until you have chosen the model you are going to use.

When we compare training data and test data, we can avoid the issue of over fitting – if your model shows good performance on the training data but not so good on the test data, you will know it is over fitting.

What Is a Hyperparameter?

In the last chapter, we mention tuning your model so let's look into it a little more. When we talk about tuning models we are actually talking about tuning the hyperparameters. Algorithms have two parameter types – the model parameter and the hyperparameter. The main distinction between them is that hyperparameters cannot be directly learned from training data whereas model parameters can.

- **Model Parameters**

A model parameter is a learned attribute used to define an individual model, for example:

- Regression coefficients

- Decision tree split locations

Model parameters can be directly learned from training data

- **Hyperparameters**

A hyperparameter will express the algorithm's high-level structural settings, for example:

- The penalty strength for regularized regression

- How many trees should be in a random forest

Hyperparameters are decided before the model is fit because they cannot be learned directly from the data.

What is Cross-Validation?

Cross-validation is a concept that will help you to tune your model. It is used for getting reliable estimates of how a model performs using just the training data.

There are a few ways that cross-validation can be done and the commonest one is called 10-fold cross-validation. This breaks the training data down into 10 equal-sized pieces, creating 10 smaller training and test data splits. The steps for this are:

1. Splitting the data into 10

2. Training the model on 9 sets

3. Evaluating it on the last set

4. Do steps two and three a total of 10 times, each time leaving a different set out

5. Average out the performance across all 10

That average is the performance estimate, or the cross-validated score and generally reliable.

Fitting and Tuning the Model

Now the dataset has been split into two sets, you know about hyperparameters an about cross-validation so now it's time to fit the model and tune it. All you need to do is the cross-validation loop in the steps above on every hyperparameter value set you want to try and the pseudo-code (high level) looks like this:

For each algorithm (i.e. regularized regression, random forest, etc.):

> For each set of hyperparameter values to try:

> > Perform cross-validation using the training set.

> > Calculate the cross-validated score.

Once the process is finished, there will be a cross-validated score for each of the hyperparameter value sets for each individual algorithm.

The next step is to choose the best hyperparameter set in each of the algorithms so:

For each algorithm:

> Retain the set of hyperparameter values that has the best cross-validated score.

> Re-train the algorithm on the whole training set (without cross-validation).

Each of the algorithms will send representatives of their own to the end selection.

Choose the Winning Model

At this stage, you will have the best model for each of the algorithms tuned using cross-validation. The important thing is that, so far, only the training data has been used.

Now we evaluate all the models and chose the best one. The test set would be saved as an unseen dataset and that means it should now be reliable in providing estimates for the performance of each model.

There are a few metrics that you can choose and, while we aren't going to spend much time on them, the rule of thumb is:

- For regression, MSE (Mean Squared Error) or MAE (Mean Absolute Error) should be used, not forgetting that lower values are best

- For classification, AUROC (Area Under ROC Curve) should be used, not forgetting that higher values are best.

This is all quite straightforward:

1. For each model, use your test set to make predictions

2. Use the predictions to calculate the performance metrics, along with the 'ground truth' target variable in the test set

Lastly, you should ask these questions to help you choose the right model:

- **Performance** – which model showed the best performance using the test set

- **Robustness** – does it show good performance over several performance metrics?

- **Consistency** – did it have a good cross-validated score using the training set?

- **Win Condition** – does it solve your business problem?

Answer those questions and you have your model.

In the next chapter, we look at the five levels of machine learning iteration.

Chapter 7

The Five Levels of
Machine Learning Iteration

Iteration is nothing more than repeating one set of tasks to get a result but then you already knew that. Most books that you read, and indeed to a certain extent, this one, will focus almost entirely on the sequential approach to machine learning – load the data, preprocess, fit the model, make the predictions, and so on.

It is a reasonable approach, that is true, but in the real world, it is rare for machine learning to be that linear. In practice, it is cyclical in nature and that commands a need for iteration, tuning, improvement, repeating the cycle over and again.

Why So Much Fuss?

Iteration is one of the core machine learning concepts and it is important on more levels than one. The first step is to understand exactly where iteration comes into the workflow – if you do, you gain many benefits:

- You will have a better understanding of your algorithms

- You will find it easier to draw up realistic project timelines

- When it comes to improving your models you will find it easier to spot the low-hanging fruit

- If your first results are not good, it helps you to maintain motivation

- You can go on to much bigger ML problems

In fact, if you look at the workflow from the iteration perspective, it can help you to see the bigger picture so, let's not waste any more time; let's look at the five levels of iteration.

The Model Level

The first iteration level is the model level and it's all about fitting the parameters. All machine learning models, no matter what type they are, are defined by multiple parameters. Feature coefficients are used to define regression models, for example, whereas branch locations are used for decision trees and weights are used to define neural networks.

But that doesn't explain how machines learn the correct values for each parameter and this is where the iterative algorithm steps in.

Using Gradient Descent to Fit Parameters

Gradient descent algorithms are hugely successful, as is the stochastic counterpart. Gradient descent is an iteration method used for finding a function's minimum. That function, where machine learning is concerned, tends to the loss function, otherwise called the cost function. Loss is nothing more than a metric used for the quantification of incorrect predictions.

The algorithm will work out what the loss is for a model with specified parameters and will then change the parameters so the loss is reduced. This process is then repeated, or iterated, until the loss cannot be reduced by any substantial amount. That last set of parameters, the ones that minimized the loss, are the ones used for defining the fitted model.

Intuition

I won't go into the math here but you do need to understand the intuition behind gradient descent:

1. First, picture a range of mountains that have valleys and hills – this is the loss function

2. Next, every location on the mountain (the set of parameters) will have an altitude – the loss

3. Now picture a ball being dropped on the mountain – this is initialization

4. Any time now the ball will roll down the steepest slope – the gradient

5. It carries on rolling – iteration – until it can roll no further because it is in a valley – the local minimum

6. Your goal is to try to find the lowest valley possible – the global minimum

There are a few neat ways that you can stop the getting caught in the local minim, for example by initializing several balls, or providing more momentum so the ball can get over the smaller hills. And if you have a bowl-shaped mountain terrain, which is a convex function, the ball will always go to the lowest point – guaranteed.

In practice, it is unlikely that you will ever need to do a from-scratch implementation of gradient descent; you are more likely to use that already exist, such as Scikit-learn.

The Micro Level

The micro level is where the hyperparameters are tuned and is often known as the model family. Think of it as being much like a broader category, where the model structures can be customized. Some of the different model families include SVMs, decision trees, neural networks, and logistic regression and each has its own structural choices that have to be made before the model parameters can be fitted.

As an example of that, take the logistic regression family. Here, separate models can be built using L1 or L2 penalties (regularization). In the decision tree family, different models can each have different choices in terms of structure, like tree depth, criteria splitting, even the thresholds for pruning. Each of these is known as a hyperparameter.

Why Are They Special?

A hyperparameter is a high0level parameter. It cannot be directly learned from data using any type of optimization algorithm. A hyperparameter provides a description of the model's structural information and that has to be determined before the parameters can be fitted.

So, when you hear that a logistic regression model is going to be trained, for example, it is actually a two-step process:

- The first step is to determine the hyperparameters, e.g., should an L or an L2 penalty be used to stop over fitting?

- The second step is to fit the parameters to your data, e.g., which model coefficients can help keep loss to a minimum?

Earlier we mentioned gradient descent, helpful in step two but, for this to be used for fitting the parameters, the user first has to set the hyperparameters.

Using Cross-Validation

I am not going to spend much time on this section because we talked about cross-validation in the last chapter. It is an iterative method that you can use to evaluate models using specific hyperparameters and is a great way of reusing training data.

Cross-validation allows you to fit your models and evaluate them using just your training data and different hyperparameter sets. This means the test set can be saved as untouched for the final selection. Refer back to the last chapter for the steps on how to use cross-validation.

The Macro Level

The third level is all about solving the problem. Very often, you will not use the first model you create because it just doesn't work. And the same will be true even after you use cross-validation. The reason for this is because fitting and tuning the hyperparameters are just two steps of the workflow surrounding problem-solving. There are some other techniques that you could use and the next two are what we call low-hanging fruit and are used for performance improvement.

Different Model Families

In machine learning, you will sometimes hear about the No Free Lunch theorem. There are several different interpretations of it but we really only care about the interpretation that states, "There is no one model family that will work best for all problems".

There are lots of factors that get taken into account such as the problem domain, data type, data sparsity, amount of data, and so on, and they all have a different effect on how different families perform.

As such, perhaps one of the best ways of improving a solution is to try it on a few model families and the pseudocode for model family selection looks like this:

training_data, test_data = randomly_split(all_data)

list_of_families = logistic regression,

decision tree,

SVM,

neural network, etc...

for model_family in list_of_families:

  best_model = tuned with cross-validation on training_data

evaluate best_model from each model_family on test_data

select final model

This is a type of nested iteration that is highly effective at problem-solving.

Ensembling Models

You can also try ensembling, i.e. putting several models together in an ensemble. One of the most common forms of this is to average the predictions from several models and, again, we talked of this in the last chapter. On occasion, you may see a minor increase in performance over one or more of the models and the following is the pseudocode needed to build the ensemble model:

training_data, test_data = randomly_split(all_data)

list_of_families = logistic regression,

      decision tree,

      SVM,

      neural network, etc...

for model_family in list_of_families:

  best_model = tuned with cross-validation on training_data

average predictions by best_model from each model_family

... profit!

Did you spot that most of this is almost identical to the last technique? That makes things easy because you can double-up on both – first, use several model families to build a good model and then ensemble all the models. Last, evaluate each model individually and evaluate the ensemble using the same test dataset.

The Meta Level

This level is all about improvement. Remember at the start, we said that better data is always going to beat fancy algorithms but that doesn't mean that more data will do the same thing. Sometimes, better data does imply that there is more data but, more often than not, the implication is that the data is clean and relevant – better features can be engineered from it.

Data improvement is also iterative and the larger the problem you tackle in machine learning, the more you will realize that getting your data right from the beginning is nigh on impossible. You may have forgotten important features, or there isn't enough data. Whatever the issue, good data scientists always have their eyes and mind open to continuous improvement.

Better Data Collection

This is a skill that will accumulate over time and experience. Whatever model you are building, you need to collect in every single piece of information that is relevant to the model, no matter how small or insignificant you think it is.

The data has to be clean, which means the minimum amount of missing data, the measurement error must be as low as possible and you should, where you can use primary metrics instead of proxies.

The Human Level

This is the final and the most important of the five levels. If you forget all that you have read so far, never forget this section. The truth is this – data science and machine learning are huge topics and for beginners it can all be quite overwhelming. There is a lot to learn and, every day, there are new developments.

Even the most experienced find it confusing at times but the human level, you, are the most important part of it all. To finish this chapter, I want to leave you with a few suggestions, just to help put things a little in perspective and lessen the overwhelming feeling.

Always Learn

Iteration is an integral part of every single machine learning layer and that is the same as your own personal skills. It is a rich field and practice really does make perfect. The more you do, the easier it will be and the better you will get.

No Perfection to Start With

Nobody can build the perfect models right from the start and it doesn't matter if your first one is bad. Personal growth is the most important part, and your focus should always be on improvement.

You Don't Need To Know It All

Nobody does, especially where machine learning is concerned. The most important thing is that you lay the foundations that help you to learn new techniques and algorithms as and when you need to use them. And yes, iteration is a part of that.

Try Everything Twice

At least twice. No matter how hard you struggle with a task or with an algorithm, no matter that you are spending way longer than you hoped on something, always try at least once more. It will be faster and much easier and you will find it much easier to monitor your own progress.

Theory, Practice, Projects – Rinse and Repeat

One of the most effective methods of learning is to go through the theory, the practice and the projects and then do it all again, this time focusing on more targeted practice and much larger projects. This way, you get to grips with theory, you develop your practical skills and you are continuously improving.

Chapter 8

Strengths and Weaknesses of Machine Learning Algorithms

In our final chapter, we are going to take some time out to look at the strengths and weaknesses of some of the modern algorithms. What we intend to do is tell you what the advantages, disadvantages, and tradeoffs for each one.

One of the trickiest things to do is to categorize the ML algorithms and there are a few approaches that you can take. For example, you can group them into supervised/unsupervised, parametric/non-parametric, and so on. If you take a look on the documentation page in Scikit -learn you can see that they use the learning mechanism to group the algorithms, producing categories like:

- Generalized linear

- Support Vector machines

- Decision Trees

- Nearest neighbor

- Neural network

- And so on

This is not necessarily a practical way of grouping the algorithms because, where applied machine learning is concerned, you generally don't stop to think about whether you are training a specific model type. Normally, all you have is your goal and your algorithm is chosen based on this. As such, there is another method of categorization approach – going by the machine learning tasks.

No Free Lunch

We mentioned this earlier – the theorem that says there isn't one algorithm best for all problems and it really means something where supervised learning is concerned. For example, you could not state that a decision tree will always work better than a neural network, or vice versa, because there are so many different factors involved, not least the size of your dataset, and the way it is structured. In short, you need to try several algorithms for every problem, ensuring you keep back a test set of untouched data for evaluating the model; then you can choose the model that fits the task best.

Obviously, you shouldn't try just any algorithm, just those that are appropriate and that is where being able to choose the right ones is important. For example, if you were cleaning house you might use a mop, a broom, or a vacuum, but you are unlikely to use a leaf blower!

Machine Learning Tasks

We're going to look at the three most important machine learning tasks – regression, classification, and clustering. Before we begin though, there are two things of note:

- We are not going to look at any adaptations that are domain-specific, like NLP (natural language processing);

- We cannot look at all the algorithms because there are simply far too many of them.

Regression

Regression comes under supervised learning for the modeling and prediction of continuous numeric variables. For example, the prediction of movements in stock price, real estate prices, or scores on student tests.

A characterization of regression tasks is that the dataset is labeled and contains a numeric target variable. In simple terms, you have what is known as ground truth, a value for every observation that can be used for supervising the algorithm.

Regularized Linear Regression

Linear regression is the commonest of all regression task algorithms and, in its most basic form, it will try fitting a straight hyperplane – nothing more than a straight line between variables. It works very well when the relationship between the two variables is linear.

In practical terms, it tends to get left behind by the regularized versions, such as Ridge, Lasso and Elastic-net. The regularization technique is used to penalize the bigger coefficients to reduce the risk of over fitting – not forgetting, the penalty strength needs to be tuned.

Strengths – it is easy to understand and is easily regularized to reduce the risk of over fitting. Plus, you can use stochastic gradient descent to update linear models with additional data.

Weaknesses - it doesn't perform very well when the variable relationships are non-linear. They also do not have the flexibility needed to capture patterns that are more complex and it can be time-consuming and not easy to add the correct polynomials or interaction terms.

Regression Tree – Ensembles

Better known as decision trees, these tend to learn hierarchically by splitting the dataset repeatedly into individual branches, each maximizing the information gain for every split. This is known as a branching structure and is what lets regression trees learn the relationships that are non-linear.

Ensemble methods include GBM (Gradient Boosted Trees) and RF (Random Forests) and they take the predictions from multiple trees and combine them. While we will not delve into the mechanics of these, it is enough to say that the random forest tends to perform highly out of the box while the gradient boosted trees are more complex to tune but have much higher ceilings for performance.

Strengths – Decision trees can easily learn the non-linear variable relationships and tend to be more robust to any outliers. Ensembles are high performers and have won a lot of ML competitions over the years.

Weaknesses – individual trees that are not constrained are more prone to over fitting; they continue to branch until they get to a stage where the training data can be memorized. However, the use of ensembles can reduce this risk.

Deep Learning

Deep learning is all about neural networks with multiple layers. These are used for learning highly complex layers and make use of hidden layers in between the inputs and the outputs. This allows them to produce intermediary data representation, something that many other algorithms find it difficult to learn.

Neural networks have a few mechanisms that are important, including drop-out and convolutions, and it these that allows them to use high-dimensional data for more efficient learning. That said, a great deal more data is required by deep learning algorithms than by any other for training purposes because they have many more parameters that need to be estimated.

Strengths – it is the most up to date and state-of-the-art algorithm for some domains, including speech recognition and computer vision. DNNs (deep neural networks) show high performance on text, audio, and image data and can be updated with additional data easily using batch propagation. The number of layers, and their structure is adaptable to multiple problem types and the fact that they have hidden layers only serves to reduce the requirement for engineering new features.

Weaknesses – these do not tend to be very suitable for use as general-purpose algorithms, simply because of the amount of data they require. Generally, tree ensembles outperform them for classical problems and they are also very expensive in computational terms to train and tuning requires a lot more expertise and experience.

Classification

Classification algorithms also fall under the supervised learning umbrella for the modeling and prediction of categorical variables. This includes prediction turnover of employees, financial fraud, spam in email, and so on. As you will soon see, many of the regression algorithms will have a classification counterpart and these have been adapted for predicting class/class probabilities rather than real numbers.

Regularized Logistic Regression

This is the linear regression counterpart and it uses the logistic function to map predictions between 0 and 1. This means that each prediction may be interpreted as a class probability.

However, the models remain linear which means they work very when a class is linearly separable – this means that a single decision interface may be used to separate them.

Strengths – each output is probabilistically interpreted and you can also regularize logistic algorithms to reduce over fitting. Models are easily updatable with additional data and, like linear regression, this is done using stochastic gradient descent.

Weaknesses – it doesn't perform well when there are a lot of decision boundaries or they are non-linear and they are inflexible when it comes to complex relationships.

Classification Trees – Ensembles

The regression tree counterpart, both tend to be called decision trees or CART – classification and regression trees.

Strengths – they are good performers and robust as far as outliers go. They are also scalable and can model the non-linear boundaries easily because they are hierarchical in structure.

Weaknesses – individual trees with no constraints are more likely to over fit by ensemble methods can be used to reduce this.

Deep Learning

Deep learning can also be adapted quite easily to classification and this does tend to be the commonest use for deep learning tasks, for example, image tasks.

Strengths – high performer in terms of audio, image and text classification tasks

Weaknesses – like the regression algorithm, DNNs need huge amounts of training data and are not good for general purpose tasks.

Support Vector Machines

SVMs or support vector machines use kernels for calculating the distance between observations. Then the algorithm will locate the decision boundary that will maximize the distance between the nearest members of the individual (separate) classes.

For example, these are much like logistic regression algorithms and, in practice, an SVMs benefits usually come from modeling decision boundaries that are non-linear, using the non-linear kernels.

Strengths – these algorithms can easily model the non-linear boundaries and you can choose from multiple kernels. They tend to be more robust to over fitting, especially when used in high-dimensional space.

Weaknesses - they use an awful lot of memory, are much harder to tune because the right kernel must be picked and, where large datasets are concerned, they do not scale very well. Usually, the SVM is discarded in favor of random forests.

Naïve Bayes

This is one of the simpler algorithms and it is based on counting and conditional probability. In essence, models are probability tables that use your training data to get updated. For new observations to be predicted, all you would do is look in the table for the class probabilities, based on the feature values. The reason it is known as naïve is that conditional independence is its core assumption – that means the input features are not dependent on one each other – and this doesn't hold true in real-world problems.

Strengths – although its core assumption doesn't tend to hold true very often, these models do perform well, mainly because they are very simple. They can be implemented easily and are scalable with the dataset.

Weaknesses – because there are so simple, other models that have been fully trained and then tunes with the algorithms we already discussed tend to beat them.

Clustering

Clustering is unsupervised and is used for finding natural groups or clusters of observations based on the dataset structure. Examples of this are groupings of similar products, customer segmentation, analysis of social networks, etc.

Because it is unsupervised, which means there isn't a right answer, we tend to use data visualization techniques for evaluation. If there are pre-labeled customers, i.e. a right answer, in the training set, classification algorithms work much better.

K-Means

An algorithm for general use, K-Means used geometric distances in between two or more points to make clusters. These are grouped, surrounding a centroid, which results in them being similar in size and globular. This is ideal for beginners because of its simplicity and flexibility, provided data is preprocessed and useful features are engineered.

Strengths – it is the most popular of all clustering algorithms because of its speed, flexibility, and simplicity.

Weaknesses – the number of clusters must be specified by the user and this isn't always going to be very easy. Plus, if there are no globular underlying clusters, K-Means will only produce bad clusters.

That was a quick look at some of the more modern algorithms for classification, regression and clustering. Before you leave, I wanted to give you some advice:

Practice, Practice, and Then Practice Some More

While reading theory about algorithms can give you a good starting point, real mastery cannot come unless you practice. Find projects and work through them; this will help you to develop your own intuition and this will lead to you being able to choose any algorithm and apply it in the right way.

Master the Basics

There are so many different algorithms and we only touched on a couple of them. There are others that can be incredibly effective if used for the right task but most are an adapted version of what is in this chapter. These will give you a very strong basis from which to go on and explore more algorithms and, when you do, don't forget – practice, practice, practice.

Remember – Better Data is Far More Effective than A Fancy Algorithm

As far as applied machine learning goes, an algorithm is nothing more than a commodity, simply because they can be swapped in and out, depending on the task. However, if your exploratory analysis is effective, you clean your data properly and you engineer the right features, your results will be so much better.

Conclusion

First of all, I want to take the time to thank you for reading my guide. I hope, as someone who wants to be a data scientist, that you found this useful. Rather than giving you reams and reams of code to learn and understand, I have gone through the process of machine learning in a matter of fact way, although as lightly as possible. I have taken you through the fundamentals of machine learning, such as:

- What machine learning is

- The different types of machine learning algorithms, including regression and classification

- Data cleansing

- The downsides of some algorithms

- The ins and outs of machine learning iteration

- Training models

- Exploratory analysis

- And much more

Obviously, the subject is far more complex than this but I have attempted to give you a decent overview with enough information to give you a good grounding.

Machine learning is complex but it is also immensely satisfying, especially when you learn just what it can lead to.

I want to wish you luck in your journey to becoming a data scientist and hope that this guide has whetted your appetite.

References

https://www.analyticsvidhya.com

https://towardsdatascience.com

https://machinelearningmastery.com

https://elitedatascience.com

https://medium.com

www.ritchieng.com

https://www.geeksforgeeks.org

https://thenewstack.io

https://www.datacamp.com

https://hackernoon.com

https://dzone.com

https://www.kdnuggets.com

https://365datascience.com